SANTA BARBARA
and BEYOND

THE PHOTOGRAPHY OF
Mike Eliason

SANTA BARBARA
and BEYOND

THE PHOTOGRAPHY OF
Mike Eliason

For my dad, who borrowed a friend's film camera
for me to take photos of the Blue Angels and opened
my eyes to the world of photography. — M.E.

Published by Beach Ball Books, a mark of Shoreline Publishing Group LLC
Santa Barbara, California
www.shorelinepublishing.com

ISBN: 978-1-936310-72-2

Designed by Patty Kelley.

Printed in Canada.
Second Edition: March 2022.

Contents

Foreword

by John Palminteri

Our eyes must see millions of images a day. Mike Eliason somehow sees them in a way that filters out some of the most amazing, precise, split-second moments on earth, and with a pulse of his fingertip, he captures them for us to see in a way we could never imagine, or may not remember.

I have known Mike for more than 30 years. As an addicted newspaper lover, I would anticipate the pages that often featured his award-winning spot news, feature, and sports photography. Then, on assignment in my role as a television and radio reporter, he was a colleague, so I could see his process and learn. You can never, however, have his same instincts.

You often only get that one chance to snap the shot of a resident fleeing a fire with the look of fear and fright in the foreground and the flames in the background. Or, an outfielder at full speed, timing the catch for the crucial out. When history is performed in the form of dancers with colorful Fiesta attire, the carefully angled shot with the dancer in front of a landmark building perfectly takes us back in time.

Mike has been able to bring all of that to the Santa Barbara community in a way that has created countless images that were clipped out to hang on a proud parent's refrigerator, or full pages framed and hanging on a wall to preserve an historic memory.

The Spirit of Fiesta dances during the Noches de Ronda at the Santa Barbara Courthouse.

He knows exactly what camera, lens, setting, position, and speed to get the shot that makes us stop and marvel at everything in front of our eyes. He gets the shots our eyes often don't see and vivid details our minds can't fully process.

How did he know the moon would rise so perfectly above that stunning Santa Ynez oak tree on the hill? How did he know the bird would swoop to a precise spot for its prey? How did he know which spectator at a parade would have the most joyous reaction?

If there was ever a way to make Santa Barbara County's mountains, sky, architecture, wildlife, events, and people even more beautiful than they already are, Mike has done it for years. When I see him on the scene, I can't help but be mesmerized at the thought of the picture he will pluck from the timeline of life and present to us all—a picture that will make us stop turning pages, stop clicking the computer, and stop moving for a moment, to view a one-of-a-kind image with amazement.

We have been getting these diamond-like nuggets in bits for years. Now we have a priceless collection to keep for many more.

John Palminteri
Santa Barbara TV and radio News Reporter/Anchor

Introduction

by Jerry Roberts

T he first time he told the visual story of Santa Barbara to the world, Mike Eliason was 19 years old, one year out of high school in Carpinteria, the small beach town where he grew up, a few miles south of the city of Santa Barbara.

Mike's school principal asked for some help with materials for a senior class trip he was leading that focused on California history and culture: Would Mike put together a selection of representative images from around Santa Barbara County?

Equipped with the Canon AE-1 Program camera he'd recently purchased at Montgomery Ward with a hundred bucks in graduation money, Eliason spent a day driving around the county, making images of iconic landmarks—the County Courthouse, Vandenberg Air Force Base, the Old Mission, the historic Franciscan church in Santa Ynez, among others—to fulfill the assignment.

His photos, along with the student tour, made their way to Sacramento, where they were assessed worthy for installation in the lobby of the state Capitol, exhibited there for several years for more than a million visitors annually, amid exhibits from California's 58 counties, as the embodiment of Santa Barbara.

A peregrine falcon hunts over a vineyard near Los Alamos.

In the intervening decades, Eliason has continuously made professional pictures with the same purpose, weaving an extraordinary and comprehensive photographic tapestry of Santa Barbara—tens of thousands of published images of its people and landscapes, celebrations and heartbreaks, architecture and critters, natural wonders and natural disasters.

A news photographer by trade, Mike is the best I ever met (during nearly half a century of working in the media industry) at the uncanny skill of capturing a single moment that shows at a glance the essence of a breaking story.

While learning his craft as a young man, he also worked for a time as a firefighter in his home town, and these days serves as the Public Information Officer for the Santa Barbara County Fire

Department. Media organizations around the world have tapped his social media feeds during wildfires and other disasters—most tragically amid the deadly 2018 Montecito debris flow—that have struck Santa Barbara in recent years.

In this collection, however, Mike brings his large talent and superb eye to a different kind of image: he defines the pictures in this book as "wild art," an old newsroom term referring to freestanding feature photos, which he's made over the last decade for his own delight and pleasure in the scenes and sights of Santa Barbara.

A winter sunset at Arroyo Burro (Hendry's) Beach.

"Something that others don't see, a slice of life of the community," is how Eliason describes the form, which not only demands powers of observation, but also artistry, resourcefulness, and perseverance.

"I do not have the patience to fish," he says. "But I can sit for ninety minutes waiting for the light to be right, or for a person to come into frame."

Born, raised, and educated in Santa Barbara, Eliason has traveled widely but always returns, forever finding new nooks, crannies, and rare beauty in explorations of home and its surroundings, from the haunting Channel Islands to the splendid Santa Ynez mountains, between them nestling the enchanting city known as "America's Riviera."

Despite Santa Barbara's global reputation as the idyllic playground of the fabulous and wealthy—thanks to a famous soap opera and to A-list residents like Oprah, Ellen, and Prince Harry—for most of its 90,000 citizens, blessed to inhabit workaday lives amid some of the most spectacular real estate on Earth, it is an unpretentious small town. So it seems fitting that its most accomplished and celebrated photojournalist is a blue-collar, local guy.

Affable, warm, and humble, Eliason is a community treasure whose mastery of composition, style, technique, and technology, combined with an encyclopedic knowledge of his subject, consistently yields photos that summon an emotional response in those who view them.

In the 1980s, Eliason's very first daily newspaper assignment was of a Saturday rummage sale at the local Unity Church; a classic "wild art" piece of newspaper business, it's the kind of mundane assignment about which many photographers would grumble, before dropping by for a drive-through, slapdash rendition.

Mike Eliason never works that way.

"You just want to show what's going on in your community, what the community is all about," he says, describing his approach.

"You've always got to come up with something—you can't say, 'I didn't get anything'—you just can't do that," he adds. "You have to come up with something and you have to be creative and you have to make it compelling."

One demonstration of Eliason's comprehensive and compendious knowledge derives from a decade he spent teaching aspiring photojournalists at Santa Barbara City College: every week, his 30 students would return with images they'd made based on the previous assignment—from portraits, sports, and news events to, yes, wild art.

In the classroom, he would display their photos on a big screen to critique them—and invariably and immediately recognize where each was taken, to the amazement of his students. It soon became a game—try to stump the professor—to come back with a photo from somewhere in Santa Barbara County that he couldn't instantly identify. It only happened once. One devious scholar finally furnished a photo that confounded him; it turned out she'd taken it in Costa Rica.

Over the years, Eliason's work has been honored with dozens of awards, from groups ranging from the National Press Photographers Association and the Associated Press to the California State Firefighters and the Pro Football Hall of Fame. His work ethic and belief in photography as public service are reflected in a commentary that referenced those awards, which he delivered to prospective photojournalists when he taught the craft:

"I was very fortunate to win a fair share of awards doing this and I always kept my trophies and my plaques hanging in my garage. So, when I get in my car, I look up, I say, 'Okay, this is what I'm capable of.' And then I went to work. And when I came home, I got out of the car and had to look up, and I said, 'Did I do that quality of work today, or did I phone it in? Did I not care, or did I do what I was capable of?'"

As you'll see on the following pages, Mike never phones it in.

Jerry Roberts is one of California's most distinguished journalists, with a 50-year career that includes a long stint at the San Francisco Chronicle *and his current work on the multimedia platform Newsmakers.*

**The Old Mission Santa Barbara
reflected in a courtyard fountain.**

Ocean

The introduction of drones has added a third dimensionality to photography, a new point of view . . . literally. Through trial and error, I have learned to A. read ALL the instructions; and B. plan ahead for the shot you hope for, because you have a very small window of time—and battery life—when shooting with a drone. You're juggling a lot of things, between the controller, the wind, the battery, so having an idea before you lift off is important. With sailboats like these, which are such a big part of the horizon in Santa Barbara, I sent the drone out while they were massing for the start of a race. I've taken pictures of this sort of scene from the land hundreds of times, but with the drone, I have the verticality that adds so much to the image. It shows the beauty of Santa Barbara from a new perspective.

Sailboats gather just off the coast before the start of one of the popular Santa Barbara Yacht Club's summertime "Wet Wednesday" races.

A pair of black skimmers search for a meal at the mouth of Mission Creek.

Following:
A fisherman enjoys the solitude near Rancho Guadalupe Dunes Preserve.

Sailboats pass a surfer catching a wave at Leadbetter Beach.

A squadron of pelicans on patrol along with a surfer welcome the new day off Santa Barbara. In the distance, the sun is just about to rise over the Santa Monica Mountains.

Winter storm waves collide at the entrance to the Santa Barbara Harbor.

A paddleboarder enjoys the pink hues of an early evening off Leadbetter Beach.

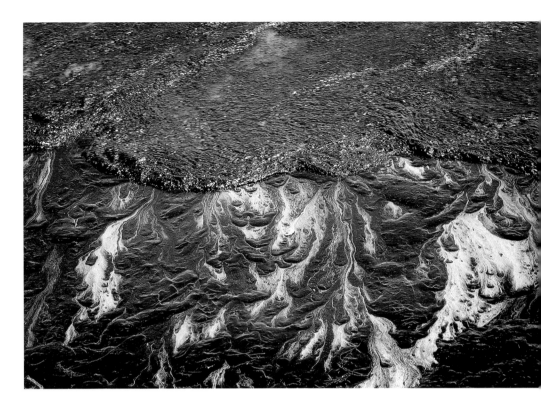

Spilled oil forms dramatic patterns after washing ashore near Refugio State Beach following a leak from a buried pipe on shore in 2015.

A humpback whale flashes its flukes as it dives in the Santa Barbara Channel near offshore oil platforms.

Following:
The sailing vessel *Sunset Kidd* cruises the Santa Barbara Channel with Santa Cruz Island in the distance.

Sunset, sails, Santa
Cruz: Santa Barbara's
Leadbetter Beach.

Right:
Waves spread out on the
shore at Hollister Beach.

Peaches, a golden retriever,
calmly rides a paddleboard
alone after her owner fell off.

A surfer takes advantage of a large winter swell at Rincon, south of Santa Barbara.

Following:
Kelp beds provide the underwater setting for a Santa Barbara sailing scene.

Above:
An egret hunts for a meal at low tide below Shoreline Park.

Left:
Sunset glows at Leadbetter Beach.

Following:
Another Leadbetter scene, as a surfer heads for breaking waves.

Nature

I took this image from the far eastern end of the East Beach volleyball courts. It was December and I knew that the sun sets behind Shoreline Park on the Mesa. You used to have to do guesswork to time photos like this, but now you have apps that show you where and when sun and moon will rise and set. I used a 600 mm lens with a doubler, so 1200 mm, and of course was looking into the sun. For my safety and for the shot, I used a film filter, like on a welder's mask, put it over the front, and shot through it. That created that black effect around the disc of the sun. As for the bird, this was the only one in the long series of images where he showed up!

Previous:
A flamingo is ready for its close-up at the Santa Barbara Zoo.

A bald eagle perched in an oak
tree in the Santa Ynez Valley.

Below:

The Santa Ynez River where it passes below Highway 154 is surrounded by fall color.

Following:

Rare for Santa Barbara, a powerful winter storm brought hundreds of lightning strikes in March of 2019. This is a 60-second timed exposure from Stearns Wharf.

The Photography of MIKE ELIASON

Above:
The King Tide floods the Carpinteria Salt Marsh Reserve, bringing an otherworldly look to the estuary.

Top left:
A pair of great horned owlets perch in a eucalyptus tree at Lake Los Carneros Park in Goleta.

Bottom left:
Snow falls atop Figueroa Mountain Road in the Los Padres National Forest.

Following:
A juvenile gray whale surfaces just off shore near Stearns Wharf.

The Photography of MIKE ELIASON

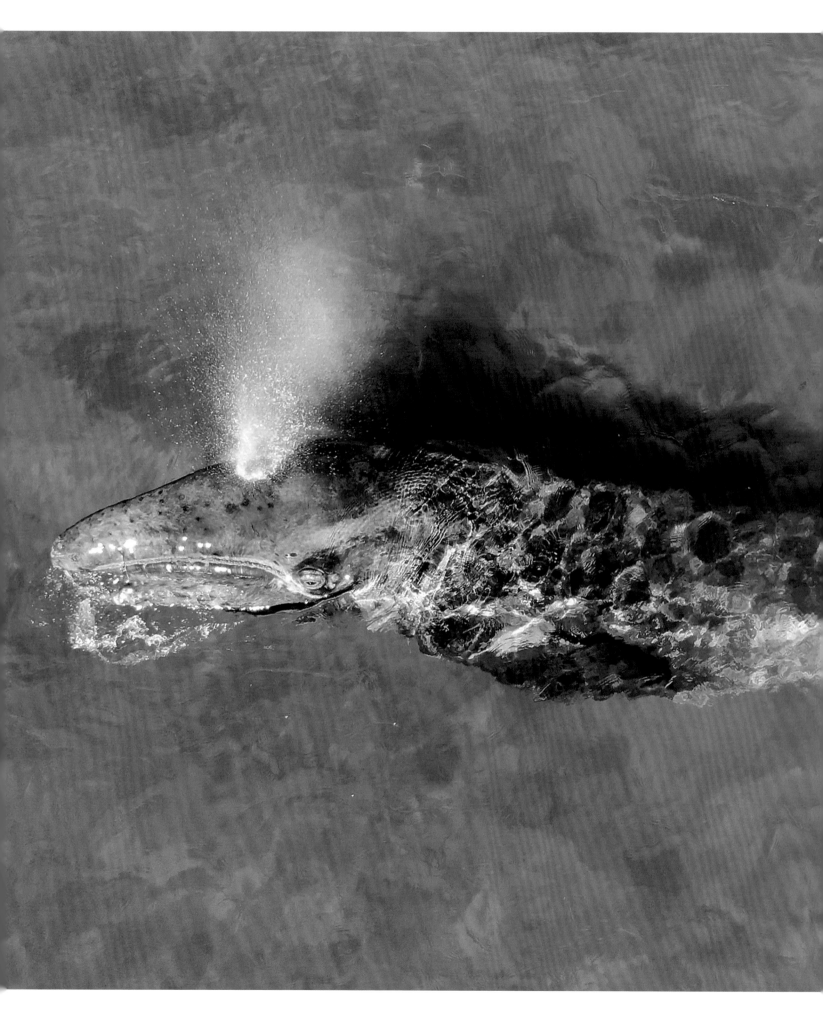

Sunset behind palm trees
in Santa Barbara's Mesa
neighborhood.

A bee abuzz doing what a
bee does in a flower along
Cathedral Oaks Road.

Above:
**A California sea lion
rests on a harbor buoy.**

Top left:
Shorebirds at low tide.

Bottom left:
**Pelicans in flight at
West Beach.**

Above:

The benefits of natural camouflage are apparent for this roadrunner.

Left:

A cloud pattern known as a mackerel sky floats high above Foxen Canyon Road in the Santa Ynez Valley.

**Morning dew collects
as drops on a spider's
web near La Mesa
Park in Santa Barbara.**

A ring formed by
atmospheric ice crystals
surrounds the moon high
above Shoreline Park.

I took a meteorology class in college, and since I'm taking pictures, and I'm the one who has to be out in the elements, it behooves me to have some knowledge of weather. So I knew that in this time of year, winter in Santa Barbara, we have very colorful sunsets. I knew high clouds were out, so that sets up for a great orange sunset. This was taken near the Bridge to Nowhere in the San Marcos Foothills Preserve. An image like this one is always a question of knowing something *might* happen, and being ready when it does.

Following:
A rare snowfall atop East Camino Cielo in the Los Padres National Forest above Santa Barbara.

Valley

Above:
**A pastoral scene in the Valley;
still life with horse.**

Right:
**The start of something good as
young grapes begin in one of the
miles of vineyards throughout
the Santa Ynez Valley.**

Previous:
**California poppies in bloom turn
a Valley hillside orange.**

Following:
**A farm's straight lines contrast
with surrounding nature on a hazy
fall afternoon in the Santa Rita Hills
between Buellton and Lompoc.**

Above:
**A drive-in screen that has seen
better days in Lompoc.**

Right:
**Storm clouds above a tree line
to the entrance of a winery off
Highway 246 near Lompoc.**

Following:
**A dusting of snow high above
the Los Padres back country,
as seen from Paradise Road.**

Above:
Colorful flowers line Alisal Road in the quaint Danish-themed City of Solvang.

Top left:
A short-eared owl on the hunt above a field.

Bottom left:
Horses graze on a hillside near Solvang.

Above:
**A tiger swallowtail atop a
colorful flower in Solvang.**

Right:
**Late winter afternoon on
a ranch road near Buellton.**

Above:
**A barn shows its age off
Sweeney Road in Lompoc.**

Left:
**An old barn along
Happy Canyon Road in
the Santa Ynez Valley.**

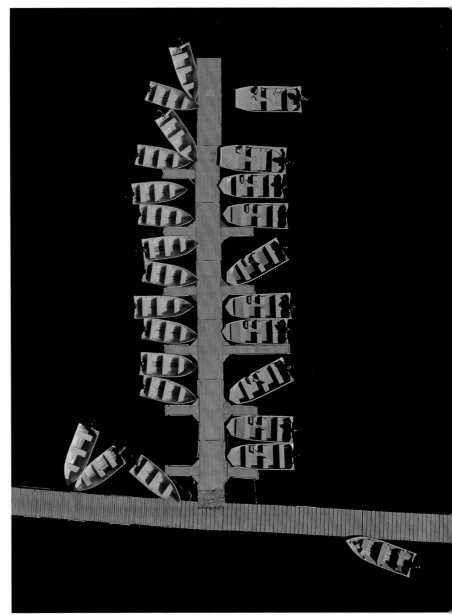

Scenes from Cachuma Lake:
The morning mist rises off
Cachuma Lake as a sculler
glides on the calm water
(left). Rental boats at a dock
as seen from above.

A carriage in front of the old
Union Hotel in Los Alamos.

A ranch off Grand Avenue in Los Olivos.

The Photography of MIKE ELIASON

When I began taking pictures, I started with black-and-white film, developing and printing my own images, so I have a nostalgic feeling for this kind of photography. I like the pureness of the way black-and-whites look. To me, these black-and-white images are a nod to Ansel Adams in a way, the purity of his landscapes. I've taken many pictures in both color and black-and-white, but sometimes, it just works better without color. Also, I'm a big puffy cloud fan! This image (left) was taken in the summer with a thunderstorm building over the mountains in the Los Padres National Forest. This scene was pretty colorful, but I think the subtleties of the spectrum of grays really jumped a little more.

Left:
**A summer storm builds
over the valley as seen from
Armour Ranch Road in
Santa Ynez.**

Above:
**A horse grazes in a paddock
off Happy Canyon Road in
Santa Ynez.**

Following:
**Fall color, Santa Ynez style.
Vineyards fade and change color
off Santa Rosa Road near Buellton.**

People
& Places

A rider takes his horse on State Street under the Highway 101
underpass during the El Desfile Historico in Santa Barbara.

Previous:
Rainbow in the rain at the Prismatic Arch.

As the morning fog lifts, a rider gets
ready for the start of the Fiesta Parade.

A colorful sunset at the start of Fiesta Pequena at the Old Mission.

Below:
A dancer is framed by palm trees during the Noches de Ronda held in the Sunken Garden at the Courthouse.

Following:
More from the Noches de Ronda, part of Santa Barbara's annual celebration of Fiesta.

Like we saw earlier, the drone provides a new point of view. Locals have all driven this road, Highway 101 through the Gaviota Pass, hundreds of times, but this gives a different view of how the road works its way through the canyon, how they built the tunnel, and how tight that space really is. Seeing this how a bird sees it reveals so much more than just driving up or down the road.

The Gaviota Pass and entrance to the 420-foot tunnel along Hwy 101 and State Route 1 that was completed in 1953.

Above:
**A full moon rises above
the Santa Ynez Mountains.**

Right:
**The Chumash Painted
Cave preserves some
of the best remaining
rock art by the Chumash
people. The area is part of
a State Historic Park.**

This is the best type of image we can take of the cave paintings made by the Chumash in the hills above Santa Barbara. The paintings are, quite properly, protected by a mesh metal fence, but there is a slightly larger opening in the fence through which I took this picture. What I also like is that it gives the image a different perspective. Ninety percent of pictures, it seems, are taken from about five feet off the ground, at eye level. This is much lower and creates a new angle of viewing. I also had to wait for just the right time in the afternoon, when the light came in just right. I'm not a big flash fan, I like natural light, so timing was the key.

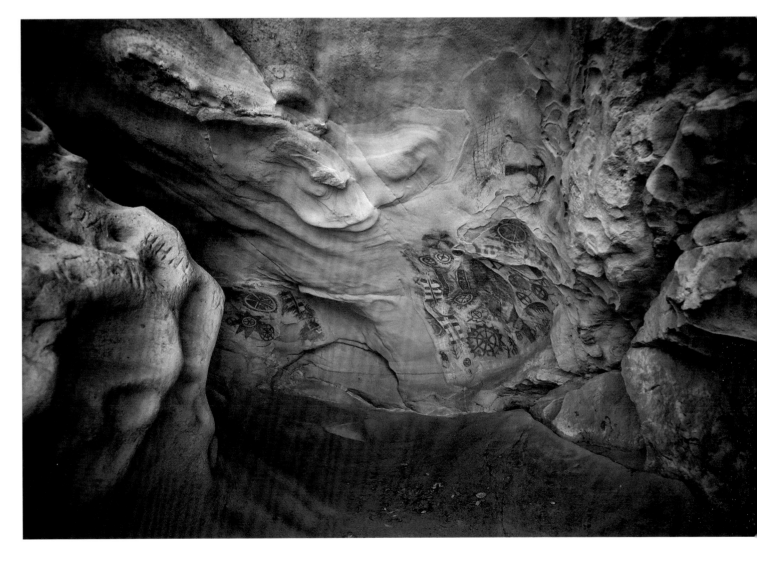

The Photography of MIKE ELIASON

Above:
A drone's-eye view of the historic Santa Barbara County Courthouse.

Right:
Colorful mosaic tiles line a staircase in the Courthouse.

Following:
As the winter sun sets, crowds scour the tide pools at low tide below Shoreline Park.

Above:

A vintage car and surfboard in Santa Barbara's revitalized Funk Zone.

Left:

A foggy night at the Santa Barbara Amtrak Station on lower State Street.

Following:

Crowds fill Shoreline Park and other beach areas to watch the Fourth of July fireworks.

The marine layer ebbs and flows during the year along the waterfront.

A woman walks in the rain along the Cabrillo Boulevard bike path.

Right:
The Bud Bottoms Dolphin Family statue, at the foot of Stearns Wharf.

Below:
Late afternoon sunlight breaks through the clouds to light the boats in Santa Barbara Harbor.

Local artists collaborate each year on colorful sculpture, costumes, and floats for the Summer Solstice Parade.

Above:
Colorful hot air balloons float above Santa Barbara's Elings Park for a fundraising event.

Left:
Getting into the swing of things at Shoreline Park in Santa Barbara.

SANTA BARBARA and Beyond

Palm trees and greenside bunkers of Sandpiper Golf Course's 11th hole next to Haskell's Beach in Goleta.

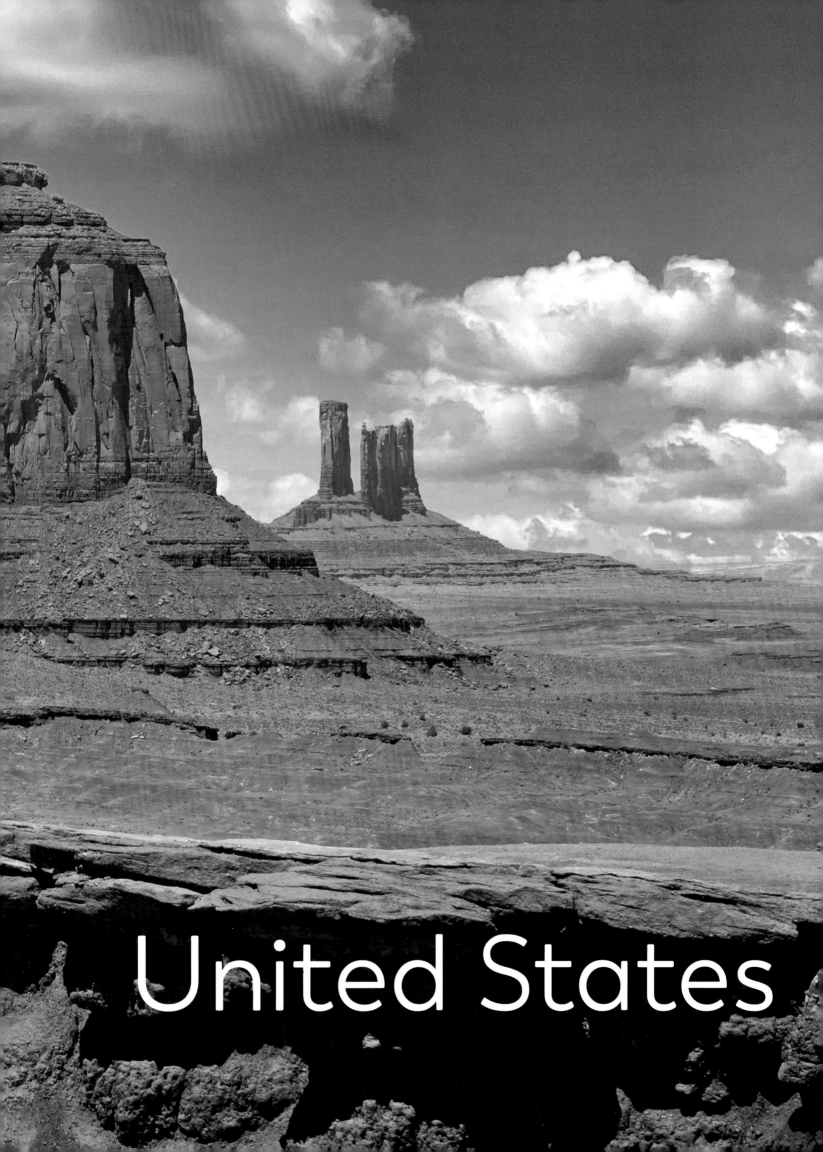

United States

Above:
**The Golden Gate Bridge
seen from Baker Beach
in San Francisco.**

Right:
**The Space Needle soars
above a Dale Chihuly glass
forest in Seattle.**

Previous:
Monument Valley, Utah.

Left:
**Saguaro cactus in
the Arizona desert.**

Bottom:
**A bit of the past remains
along old Route 66 in
Holbrook, Arizona.**

Scenes from National Parks:
A gnarled pine at Olmsted Point (right) and El Capítan (far right), both in Yosemite. Bison walk through snow along the Fire Hole River in Yellowstone (below).

Above:
**Norris Geyser Basin
in Yellowstone National Park.**

As noted in the dedication, I got into photography because I wanted to take pictures of the Blue Angels air show. Since then, I've flown in jets and sailplanes and blimps and everything in between. This image (right) was taken on the island of Hawaii during an eruption of Mount Kilauea in 2018. We were in an open helicopter, doors off, hovering a couple hundred feet above the lava. And you could feel the heat, you could smell lava. As for shooting from the air, you have to think ahead about what you're hoping to get, how you want to frame or expose the shot. When you're flying, you might not get a second chance.

Above:
**Silver Cascade waterfall,
in New Hampshire.**

Top right:
**A carpet of color creates quite a
crunch for leaf peepers admiring
the fall color of New England.**

Bottom right:
**A Vermont sugar shack,
used in making maple syrup.**

Three scenes from the former 19th century gold-mining ghost town of Bodie, near the California-Nevada border off Highway 395.

Following:
Clouds and contrails from crisscrossing aircraft fill the sky above Palm Springs.

Right:
**Sunrise in Hawaii:
A surfer heads out
before sunrise at
Kahanamoku Beach.**

Below:
**A surfer and his
board are a splash of
color at world-famous
Waikiki Beach.**

Washington, D.C.: The Peace Monument near the U.S. Capitol honors sailors who died in the Civil War (opposite top); the Lincoln Memorial (opposite bottom); the Marine Corps War Memorial (above) in Arlington, Virginia.

International Sights

Above:
Big Ben in London.

Right:
**A sentry guards the crown
jewels at the Tower of London.**

Previous:
**Sunset from Piazzale
Michelangelo, Florence, Italy.**

**A filter gives this image of a
Le Stryge (a statue of a chimera
atop Notre Dame in Paris) a
vintage Victor Hugo look.**

In the Bahamas,
a green sea turtle
comes in for a look
(above), and waves
lap on a beach under
Atlantic skies (right).

Stingrays, sea stars, and stunning sea views are part of a trip to the Cayman Islands.

Following:
A 12-foot Great White Shark comes in for a close-up in the waters of Guadalupe Island, Mexico.

I enjoy seeing different parts of the world, how people live, and capturing those places differently. That's the challenge for me, to come up with something we've all seen before but with my take on it. This trip to Cuba had great meaning to me in particular, having been raised during the Cold War and read about this in history books, to actually see and experience this culture. Every picture has been taken—it's just a question of finding your own spin on that subject. And I hope that's what I was able to do here and throughout my travels.

Scenes from Cuba: Tourists and locals enjoy the seawall known as the Malecón (opposite); vintage American cars are a familiar sight in Havana (left and above).

Following:
Pirates of the Caribbean? The *Jolly Roger*, a privateer-turned-tourist ship, sails the waters off Grand Cayman Island.

Acknowledgments

I'd like to thank a few people. First of all, thank you for purchasing this book. It means a lot to me that I can take a photo and have it end up meaning so much to people.

- » Thank you for spending part of your day looking at my photos on social media because I know there is a lot to look at out there, and for all of the kind notes and messages.
- » Thank you to Len Wood and Steve Malone for the years of encouragement.
- » Thank you to my fire family for the welcome and support.
- » Thanks to Jim Buckley and Patty Kelley for all of their help and ideas with getting this book published.
- » And finally, thank you to my family and to my wife, Kathy, for the patience while waiting for me to take the photos.

—Mike Eliason

ELIASONPHOTOS

For our part, thanks to Mike, of course, for his diligence and talent (and patience!). He and Patty worked very hard to sort through his thousands of images to choose just the right ones for this book. Thanks to the folks at Chaucers and all local bookstores and gift shops for helping readers find Mike's book. Thanks to the *Independent* for its support.

If you'd like to order additional copies of Mike's book, please visit us at www.shorelinepublishing.com.

Many thanks.

—James Buckley Jr., Shoreline Publishing Group LLC

Mike Eliason

Award-winning photographer Mike Eliason has more than 35 years experience behind the lens working with Santa Barbara-area media companies. His career includes more than two dozen honors from the Associated Press, California Newspaper Publishers Association, The New York Times Company, National Newspaper Publishers Association, Pro Football Hall of Fame, and the International Association of Firefighters.

Mike's work has been seen around the world, picked up by media platforms such as ABC, CBS, NBC, CBC, BBC, Fox News, CNN, MSNBC, *The New York Times*, *Los Angeles Times*, *Wall Street Journal*, *USA Today*, *Time*, *People*, and *Sports Illustrated*.

Mike was also a reserve firefighter for the Carpinteria-Summerland Fire Department for eight years, and since 2012 has been a Public Information and Education Officer for the Santa Barbara County Fire Department. Mike also taught photojournalism at Santa Barbara City College, was a contributing photographer for the National Football League, and even got to fly with the US Navy Blue Angels.

He was raised in Carpinteria, California, and lives in Santa Barbara with his wife, Kathy.